Starting off with
Time

Written by Peter Patilla

Illustrations by Liz Pichon

BARRON'S

First edition for the United States and its dependencies published 2001
by Barron's Educational Series, Inc.

Originally published 2000 by Oxford University Press.

Text © Peter Patilla 2000
Illustrations © Liz Pichon 2000

The moral rights of the author and illustrator have been asserted.

All inquiries should be addressed to:
Barron's Educational Series, Inc.
250 Wireless Boulevard
Hauppauge, New York 11788
http://www.barronseduc.com

International Standard Book No. 0-7641-1660-6

Library of Congress Catalog Card No. 00-190710

PRINTED IN HONG KONG
9 8 7 6 5 4 3 2 1

My name is

....

Notes for parents and teachers

This book develops early concepts of *time* for adults and children to enjoy and share together. It has been carefully written to introduce the key words and ideas related to *time* that children will meet in their first couple of years in school.

Throughout the book, you will see **Word Banks** that contain the new math terms introduced for each concept. All the words from the word banks are gathered together at the back of the book. You can use the word banks with your child in several ways:

- See which of the words are recognized through games such as *I spy: I spy the word "clock"—can you find it? I spy a word beginning with "h"—where is it?*
- Choose a word and ask your child to find it in the book.
- Let your child choose a word from the word bank at the back of the book, and say something about it.

Look for other opportunities in everyday life to use the ideas and vocabulary introduced in this book. Include time words such as: quick, slow, early, late, before, and after. Ask questions such as: What did we do this morning? What did we do yesterday? Make sure that children realize that math is easy, and most importantly, fun.

A day

Each day ends at midnight.
A new day starts just after midnight.

Midnight is the time between one day and the next.
Midday is the middle of the day. It is also called noon.

Some people work during the night.
Who could they be?

Word Bank

- day
- night
- midnight
- midday
- noon

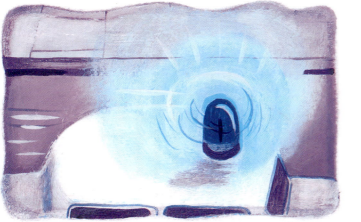

Do you know of any animals that come out at night?

A week

Each week has seven days.

Here are the names for each day of the week.
The diary shows what Joe did each day in one week.

Monday

school visit

Tuesday

birthday party

Wednesday

swimming club

Thursday

visited Grandma

Friday

cleaned my bedroom

Saturday

went shopping

Sunday

went to the park

We call Saturday and
Sunday **the weekend**.

Today

Wednesday

What day was it yesterday?

Today

Sunday

What day will it be tomorrow?

Word Bank

day

weekend

diary

today

week

tomorrow

yesterday

weekday

Which are weekend days?
Which are weekday days?
What day is it today?

Monday	Tuesday	Wednesday	Thursday	Friday	Saturday	Sunday

A year

A year is divided into months, weeks, and days.

A year has: 12 months
52 weeks
365 days

Every fourth year has one day more. This is called a leap year. Leap years have 366 days.

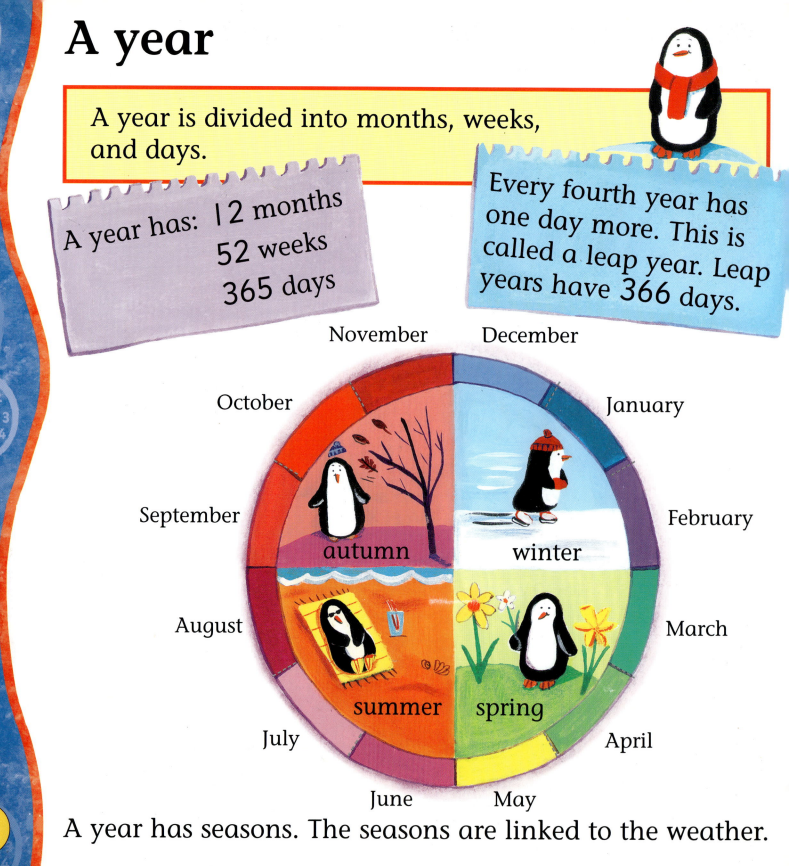

A year has seasons. The seasons are linked to the weather.

Which seasons do you think these belong to?

In which month is your birthday?
How old are you?
How old will you be next year?

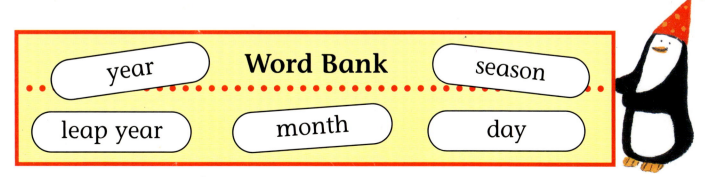

Word Bank

year   season   leap year   month   day

Getting older

As time passes things get older.

Seeds grow into plants.
It can take a few
months or
many years.

Eggs hatch into birds.
It usually takes a few weeks.

Babies eventually become
adults. It takes about
18 years.

Which of these are new?

How old will each person be next year?

Word Bank

young

old

new

older

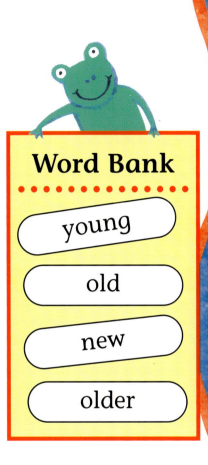

Which is the baby and which is the adult?

Hours, minutes, and seconds

A day is divided into hours, minutes, and seconds.

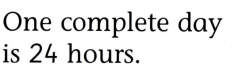

midnight

12 hours | 12 hours

midday

One complete day is 24 hours.

It takes one hour for the big hand to move right around a clock. One hour is 60 minutes.

A minute is divided into seconds. There are 60 seconds in one minute. A second is a very short time.

12
11
1
10
2
9
3
8
4
7
5
6

a minute

Which of these would you time in:

- hours?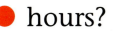
- minutes?
- seconds?

sleeping

drawing a picture

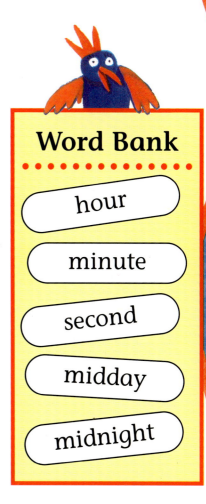

Word Bank

hour

minute

second

midday

midnight

writing your name

brushing your teeth

drinking a cup of milk

watching TV

13

Clocks and watches

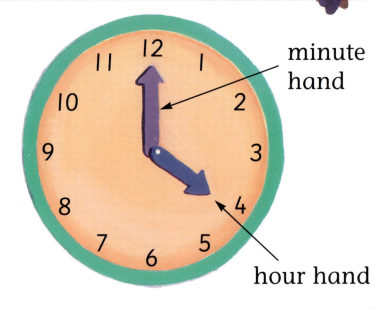

Clocks and watches tell us the time.

Some clocks and watches have hands. The big hand tells the minutes. The small hand tells the hours.

minute hand

hour hand

second hand

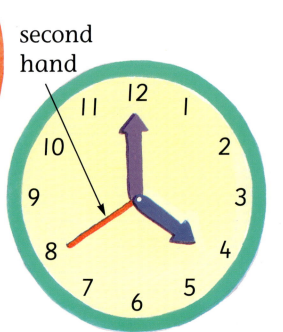

Some clocks and watches have a special hand that tells the seconds. This moves around quite quickly.

Some clocks and watches do not have hands. They have only numbers. These are called digital clocks and watches.

What is special about these clocks and watches?

What does this do in the morning?

Which noise might you hear from this clock?

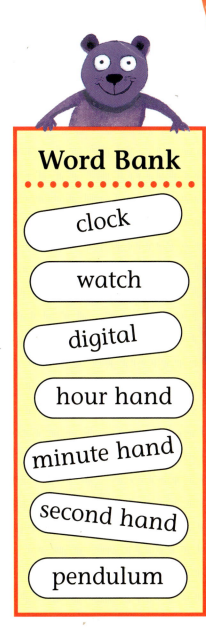

Word Bank

- clock
- watch
- digital
- hour hand
- minute hand
- second hand
- pendulum

What is a pendulum?

Why is a nurse's watch upside down?

What makes a digital watch work?

Digital time

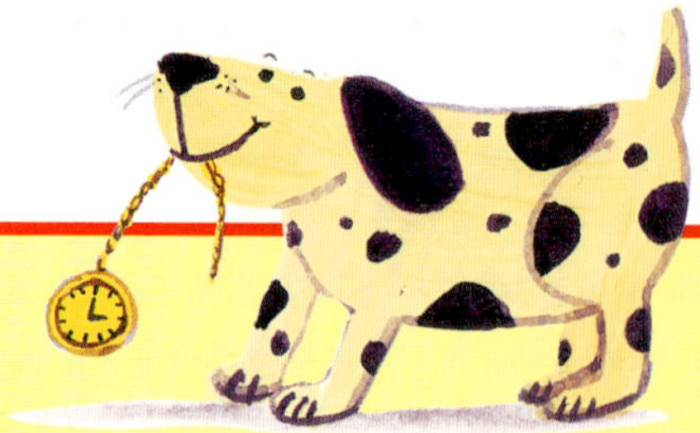

Digital clocks and watches use numbers to tell the time.

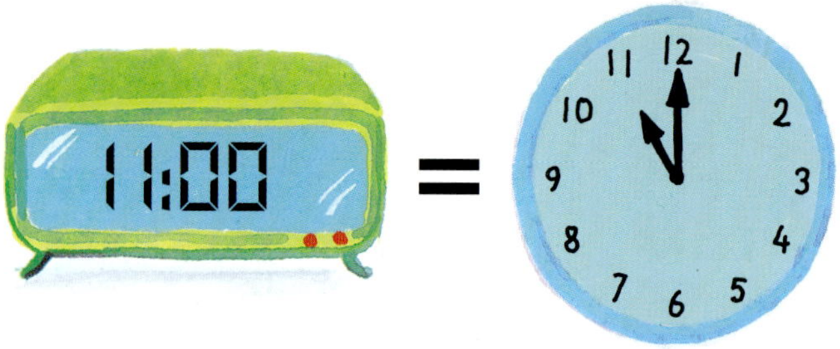

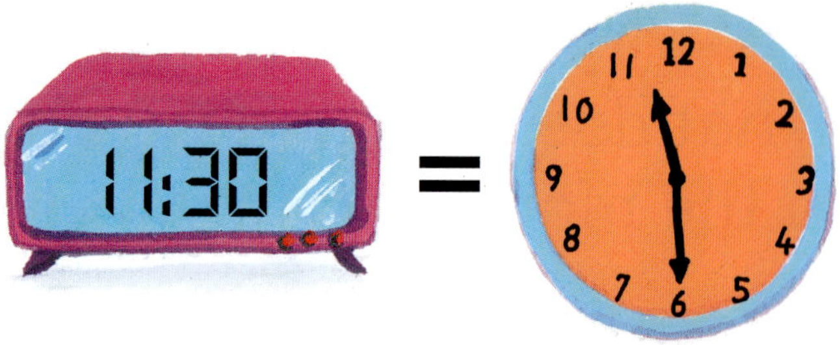

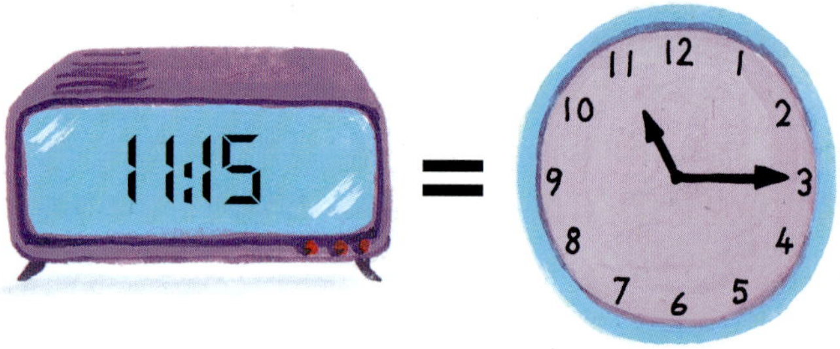

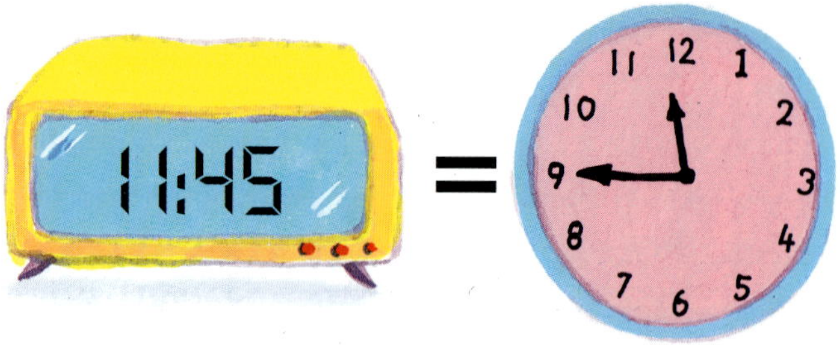

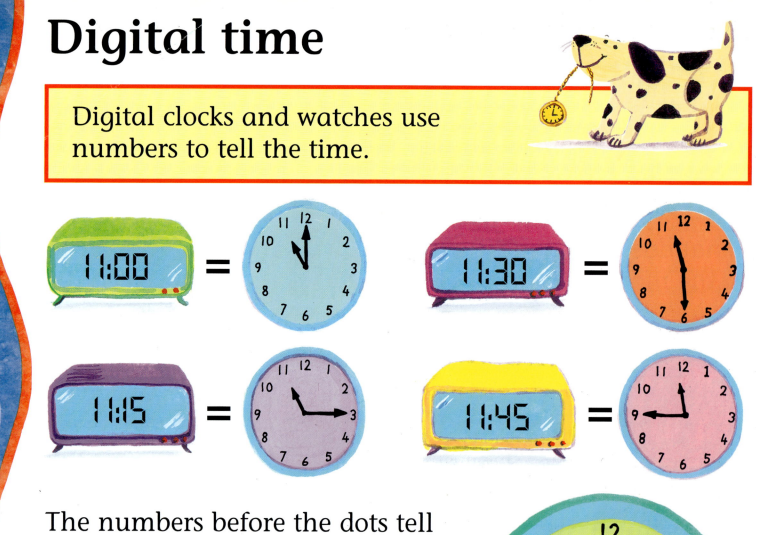

The numbers before the dots tell you the hour.
The numbers after the dots tell you the minutes past the hour.

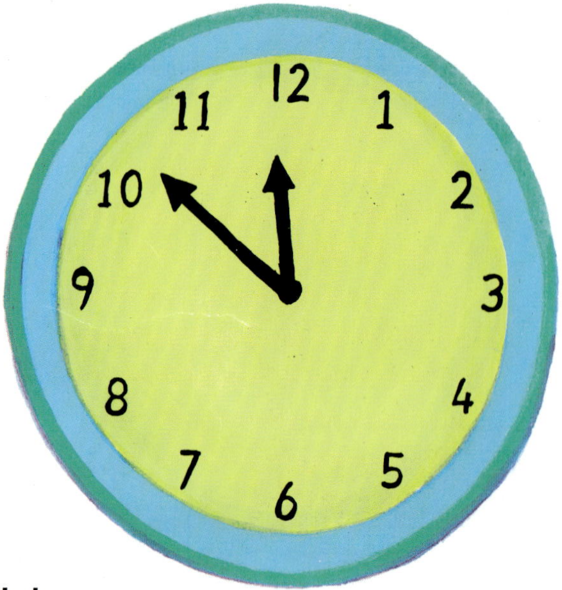

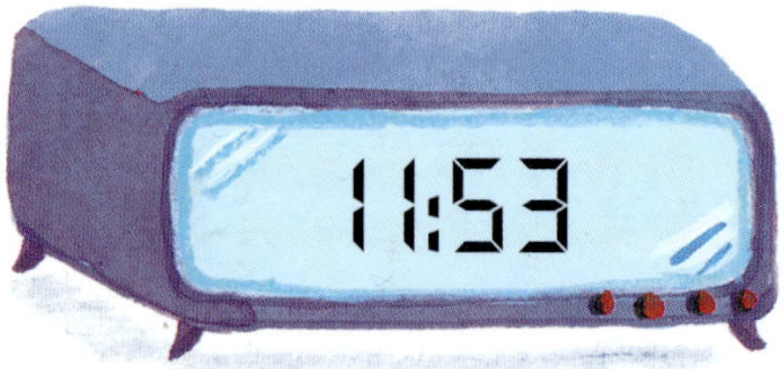

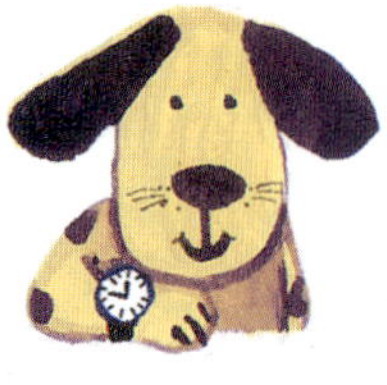

Both clocks show 53 minutes past 11.
We say this time as eleven fifty-three.

Here are some morning times.
Which is the earliest time?
Which is the latest time?

How many minutes did it take to paint the picture?

Word Bank

digital

hour

minute

earliest

latest

past

On the hour

When the minute hand is on 12, it is something o'clock. The hour hand says which o'clock.

All these times are o'clock times.

O'clock times on digital clocks and watches end in 00.

9 o'clock

12 o'clock

Is she late for school?

Is he going to bed early?

At what time is she eating?

At what time is he playing?

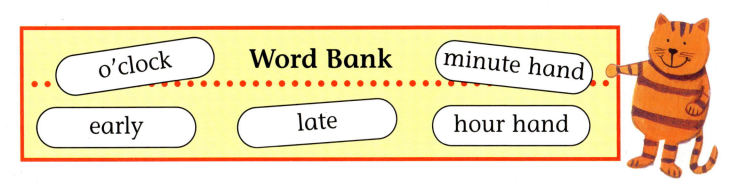

o'clock   **Word Bank**   minute hand

early   late   hour hand

Morning, afternoon, evening

Each day has parts called morning, afternoon, and evening.

Evening is from about dinnertime until we go to bed.

Nighttime is when we are asleep in bed.

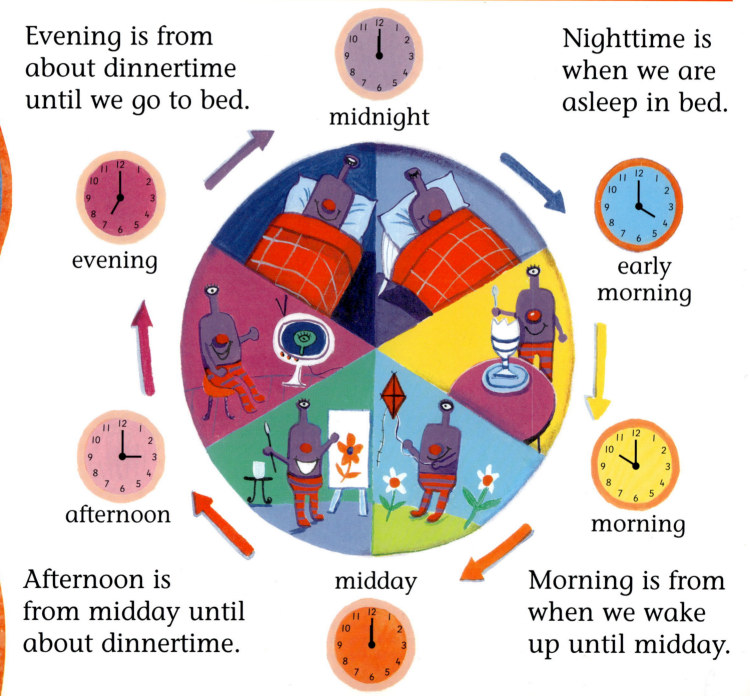

midnight

evening

early morning

afternoon

morning

Afternoon is from midday until about dinnertime.

midday

Morning is from when we wake up until midday.

Here is what Zig and Zog did one day.

Zig

Zog

Who went shopping in the morning?
Who had a picnic lunch?
Who wore red pajamas in the evening?
What do you like doing in the evening?

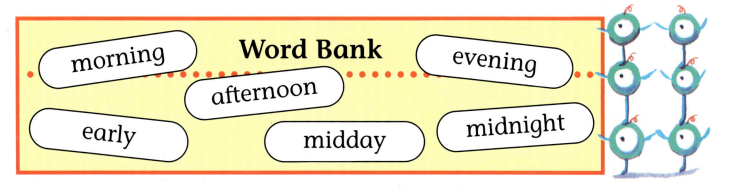

morning
afternoon
early
Word Bank
midday
evening
midnight

Half past

When the minute hand is on 6, the time says half past. The hour hand is halfway between two different o'clock times.

All these times are half past times.

Half past times on digital clocks and watches end in 30.

half past nine or nine thirty

half past twelve or twelve thirty

At what time is each thing happening?

Minutes past

There are 5 minutes between each number on a clock face.

5:50 is nearly 6 o'clock, so the hour hand is near the 6.

Can you find pairs of clocks that show the same time?

Did you know?

The ancient Romans used the moon to help plan their calendar.

The ancient Egyptians used the sun to help plan their calendar.

Hundreds of years ago water clocks were used. Water dripped from one bowl into another. The level of water showed the time.

Candles were used as early clocks. Marks down the side showed how long the candle had been burning.

Hourglasses have been used for hundreds of years to time how long things take.

Sundials were another way to tell the time. They only work in the daytime and when the sun shines.

Telling the time accurately only became necessary when trains were invented. Clocks were put on important buildings so that everyone could tell the time.

Word Bank

night

midnight

day

noon

afternoon

evening

morning

midday

today

morning

tomorrow

Word Bank

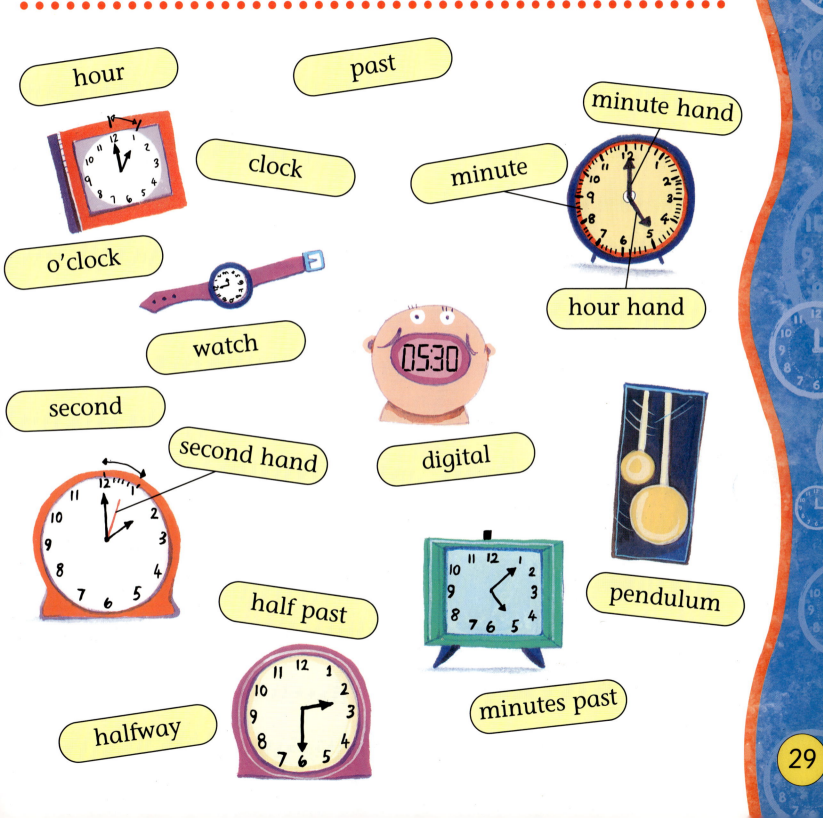

hour

past

minute hand

clock

minute

hour hand

o'clock

watch

second

second hand

digital

half past

pendulum

halfway

minutes past

Word Bank

late

nearly

early

latest

earliest

old

older

new

young

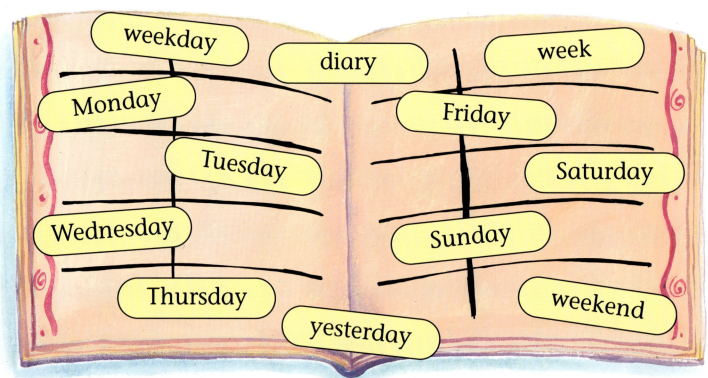

weekday

diary

week

Monday

Friday

Tuesday

Saturday

Wednesday

Sunday

Thursday

weekend

yesterday

30

Word Bank

month

year

season

January

February

March

April

May

June

July

August

September

October

November

December

leap year

Time Puzzle

Match each picture to a time.

8:45

11:00